5513 1287

Little Brown Bats

by Joyce Markovics

Consultant: DeeAnn M. Reeder, PhD
Associate Professor, Department of Biology
Bucknell University
Lewisburg, Pennsylvania

BEARPORT
PUBLISHING

New York, New York

Credits
TOC, © Mc Donald Wildlife Photog./Animals Animals; 4–5, © Mc Donald Wildlife Photog./Animals Animals; 5, © suradech sribuanoy/Shutterstock; 6, © Oliver Sved/Shutterstock; 6–7, © AP Photo/The Olympian; 8, © Scientifica/Visuals Unlimited, Inc.; 8–9, © Merlin D. Tuttle, Bat Conservation International; 10, © John M. Burnley/Science Photo Library; 11, © Ted Kinsman; 12–13, © AP Photo/Amy Smotherman Burgess; 14–15, © U.S. Fish and Wildlife Service; 16–17, © E.R. Degginger/Alamy; 18–19, © Joe McDonald/Visuals Unlimited, Inc.; 20–21, © Minden Pictures/SuperStock; 22L, © Mc Donald Wildlife Photog./Animals Animals; 22R, © michaeljung/Shutterstock; 23TL, © Ted Kinsman; 23TR, © Jiri Vaclavek; 23BL, © Oliver Sved/Shutterstock; 23BR, © Igor Chernomorchenko/Shutterstock.

Publisher: Kenn Goin
Senior Editor: Joyce Tavolacci
Creative Director: Spencer Brinker
Design: Debrah Kaiser
Photo Researcher: We Research Pictures, LLC

Library of Congress Cataloging-in-Publication Data

Markovics, Joyce L., author.
    Little brown bats / by Joyce Markovics ; consultant: DeeAnn M. Reeder, PhD.
        pages cm. — (In winter, where do they go?)
    Includes bibliographical references and index.
    ISBN 978-1-62724-315-5 (library binding) — ISBN 1-62724-315-1 (library binding)
    1. Little brown bat—Juvenile literature. 2. Little brown bat—Hibernation—Juvenile literature. 3. Bats—Juvenile literature. I. Title.
    QL737.C595M366 2015
    599.4—dc23
                                        2014004649

For more information, write to Bearport Publishing Company, Inc., 45 West 21st Street, Suite 3B, New York, New York 10010. Printed in the United States of America.

10 9 8 7 6 5 4 3 2 1

Contents

Little Brown Bats

In fall, a little brown bat soars through a forest.

Its furry body is fat.

It has been eating all summer.

The bat is getting ready for winter.

Little brown
bats eat **insects**, such
as moths, in summer.
During winter, there are
fewer insects
to eat.

moth

The bat looks for a place to spend winter.

It searches for a dark cave.

To find one, it may fly up to 100 miles (161 km).

Sometimes, little brown bats spend winter in empty **mines**.

Finally, the tiny bat spots a cave.

It sees many other bats flying nearby.

Together, they swoop inside the cave.

cave

Thousands of bats may use the same cave.

The bats fly to the ceiling of the cave.

They grip it with their feet.

Then they hang upside down!

hooked claws

Bats have hooked claws. This helps them hang from their feet.

To keep from freezing, the bats bunch together.

They do not eat for many months.

Spending the winter in this way is called **hibernation**.

The bats stay in the cave for up to seven months.

13

How do the bats **survive** all winter?

They live off the food stored in their bodies.

They get water by licking drops off the cave walls.

The bats also lick water drops that form on their fur.

water drops

In early spring, the bats warm up.

They come out of hibernation.

They stretch their wings.

After hibernating, the bats are very hungry.

The bats leave their winter home.

Flowers bloom outside the cave.

Insects buzz all around.

In warm weather, the bats sleep in barns, attics, or trees.

After not eating all winter, the bats start hunting.

They fly into the warm night sky chasing after bugs.

moth

In spring, summer, and fall, bats sleep during the day. They hunt at night.

Little Brown Bat Facts

There are about 1,300 different kinds of bats around the world. Little brown bats live in North America.

Where little brown bats live

Food: Insects, such as moths, wasps, beetles, mosquitoes, and flies

Size: 2.5 to 4 inches (6.1 to 10 cm), with a wingspan of 9 to 11 inches (23 to 28 cm)

Weight: ⅛ to ½ ounce (3.5 to 14 g)

Life Span: 6 to 30 years

Cool Fact: Little brown bats' wings are covered with stretchy skin.

Size of an adult little brown bat

Glossary

hibernation (hye-bur-NAY-shuhn) spending the winter in a cold, inactive state

insects (IN-sekts) small animals that have six legs, two antennae, three main body parts, and a hard covering

mines (MYENZ) deep holes or tunnels in the ground made by people from which coal and minerals, such as gold, are taken

survive (sur-VIVE) to stay alive

Index

Read More

Bash, Barbara. *Shadows of the Night: The Hidden World of the Little Brown Bat.* San Francisco: Sierra Club (2004).

Carney, Elizabeth. *Bats.* Washington, D.C.: National Geographic (2010).

Markle, Sandra. *Bats: Biggest! Littlest!* Honesdale, PA: Boyds Mills Press (2013).

Learn More Online

To learn more about little brown bats, visit
www.bearportpublishing.com/InWinterWhereDoTheyGo?

About the Author

Joyce Markovics lives along the Hudson River in Tarrytown, New York. She enjoys spending time with furry, finned, and feathered creatures.